WHAT PEOPLE ARE SAYING ABOUT

FACING THE

This is a book for those times when you are literally on your knees and the screaming inside your head is so loud that it's either going to come out, or tear you apart. And for those times when you are numb to the marrow of your bones and the despair is so overwhelming that you can see no way to keep going. There's very little that can help a person in those places, as you will know if you've been there or tried to help someone going through that kind of deep depression. Cat Treadwell has written a book that faces the torment head on, and offers words of support and insight to help a person not be destroyed by what is happening to them. A brave, raw and potent piece of writing, from someone who knows that the dark nights cannot be magically banished, but that they can be survived.

Nimue Brown, Author of *Druidry & the Ancestors*

It takes a certain special something for words in a book to reach you through a tar-pit of depression – the words in this book have that something. Cat shares her own experience and that of others simply and sensitively, offering insights and suggestions in small doses which have helped sufferers to hold on when it is hardest to do so. Some books expect a lot from you – this one accepts you where you are, as you are, offering perspective and a safe place to be when you're vulnerable. If the best in us comes out when we are tested, maybe these words will guide you to the best in you.

Paul C. Newman, Bard & Storyteller
www.storyfolksinger.co.uk

Facing the Darkness

Facing the Darkness

Cat Treadwell

Winchester, UK
Washington, USA

First published by Moon Books, 2013
Moon Books is an imprint of John Hunt Publishing Ltd., Laurel House, Station Approach,
Alresford, Hants, SO24 9JH, UK
office1@jhpbooks.net
www.johnhuntpublishing.com
www.moon-books.net

For distributor details and how to order please visit the 'Ordering' section on our website.

Text copyright: Cat Treadwell 2013

ISBN: 978 1 78099 900 5

A CIP catalogue record for this book is available from the British Library.

Design: Lee Nash

Cover art: © Tom Brown, www.hopelessmaine.com

Artwork: © Emma Hotchkin

Printed and bound by CPI Group (UK) Ltd, Croydon, CR0 4YY

We operate a distinctive and ethical publishing philosophy in all
areas of our business, from our global network of authors to
production and worldwide distribution.

CONTENTS

How to Read This Book   x

Acknowledgements   xi

Introduction   1

The Deep Darkness   5

The Whirlwind   29

The Raging Fire   41

The Rushing Torrent   61

Spirit   84

For Jim. The hand that holds mine in the dark.

How to Read This Book

When you're in the Dark places, it's not easy to undertake involved exercises, deep meditation or even simple focus.

This book is intended to be read in small doses. Find a page that you can read through and absorb. That's enough.

Small sections, highlighted in **bold,** offer ideas to actively distract, come back to yourself, simply cope – if you are able. Take these at your own pace, but do try.

I've divided the 'chapters' into sections, based around the elements – those wild forces that make us what we are, ebb and flow, nourish and destroy.

Let these stories distract when needed, as a guidebook and companion, engaging your mind and spirit. You're not alone on this path, and it doesn't end here.

Others are with you. You'll see their stories too, here and there among the pages. Allow them to accompany you along the way.

Acknowledgements

Although one of the loneliest experiences that it is possible to undertake, no book is truly written in isolation.

My deepest thanks go to those who have helped with the work you hold here now – whether it be with ideas, thoughts, experiences or stories told from the darkest of places. Please know that you are honoured more deeply than I can ever adequately convey.

And to those who have held me up, throughout it all – and who will probably do so again.

Introduction

We all have a Dark Side. Like the Moon, it exists just out of sight for some of the time, but then turning slowly to engulf us – or suddenly being noticed, overwhelming us with its weight, stifling every 'light' thought, positive feeling or shred of confidence that we thought we could rely on. Our foundation is shaken, truths revealed.

Fairytales have told us for years how to deal with our own personal darkness. Find its true name. Face it, armed and ready, even if the odds are a million to one. Ultimately, it's about confidence in yourself and being able to stand up to what might be hidden inside, ready to jump out. And that Thing knows your own weaknesses, can embody your fears, insidiously reaching straight to the root of your own Self and (apparently) preparing to rip it out ...

Rationally, this isn't actually true. Your subconscious isn't trying to destroy you. But malfunctions, misunderstandings, whether in physical chemistry or mental and emotional experience, can make it seem that this is the case.

As Pagans, we realise that giving up, succumbing to the blackness, dying – none of it is as final a cut-off as we might think. There's more to life's path, and this is just one element, one experience to be lived through, learned from. Life is a series of challenges; it's not unreasonable that some will be harder than others. This isn't a game and the odds aren't stacked in our favour.

But it's hard to think rationally when you're suffering.

The modern world can be harsh, overwhelming – often insane. As humans, we're slowly learning what's needed, and some families, communities, groups of friends come together to support those who fall. Healing the mind, though, is far harder than healing the body and much less understood. It's hard to pin down subjective experience, especially when it's perceived as irrational, mad, lunatic.

I write these words not as a professional counsellor or psychiatrist, but as a fellow sufferer. I've walked the dark paths, and still do. As part of a wider community, I want to reach out with my tale and some lessons learned along the way, to hopefully help others as they explore, cutting their own route through the forest, shining a glimmer of hope and companionship into that terrible pit of despair, the screams of rage and pain allowing a song to be heard.

As a Druid, a modern Pagan, I believe firmly that our spirituality is ingrained into our lives, in good times and bad. We don't always feel like casting a circle. We don't always have the energy to get out and actively help ourselves. But we are part of that wider world, living creatures on this planet, and so surrounded *wherever we are* by others who may help, or even simply distractions to get us through, to cut through the noise and remind us who we are.

If we don't allow it to overwhelm us, the Dark places can be a refuge, a point of quiet in a busy life, a place of inspiration. These are the teachings of our ancestors, as we draw magic from the mysterious cauldron, weave a web to catch and protect us, draw on the relationship of shared story and experience to nourish us and keep us going. Or just sit and allow tears to flow, wailing to be heard, experience to be felt without judgement or medication.

Walk with me into the dark woods. We move forward together.

This can only ever be my story – each experience is so deeply subjective that I have no way of knowing how relevant it will be to a given reader.

I offer this book as my sacrifice, hard-earned in body and spirit, so that something good may come from a time of intense suffering, loss, confusion and disconnection.

My sincere hope is that it can help, even if in the smallest of ways.

We all walk the dark paths. Please know that we do not have to do so alone.

The Deep Darkness

Facing the Darkness

Run so far and so long
Run out of all care to fight
Run and hide away

Hide that you hate you
Hide in deepest darkest hole
Hide your soul away

Soul in pain cries out
Soul to the universe sings
Soul must see her face

Face to face you cry
Face the dark and cry your name
Face the dark and smile

Smile, you are held fast
Smile, your fear is meaningless
Smile at your new face

Jess

Earth

*Earth's crammed with heaven ... But only he who sees, takes off his
shoes. – Elizabeth Barrett Browning*

No matter where we stand, the Earth is always beneath us,
holding us up, catching us when we fall. It can hold us in its thick
mud as we sob, or provide the bump that we need to clear our
heads.

Or sometimes we just need to sit.

Go outside, to somewhere safe and natural – a park, garden,
wood or hill. Even a little grass and a tree is fine.

Sit on the earth. Reach into it, feeling the grass, touching the
dirt. Place your hands, palms down, onto the ground. Truly feel
it, the land beneath you.

Are you high up, or closer to sea level? In the countryside or
a busy city? What's beneath you – a subway, plumbing and
drains, or rabbit warrens and worms? Imagine it, your busy
surroundings. Look around. How much of it can you see?

Is it sunny and warm out there, encouraging growth and
reaching upwards? Or wet, as the earth slowly becomes
saturated and your own hair and skin starts to drip along with
the leaves?

Root down, if you can. Feel yourself extending into the
earth, through fingers, toes or bones. You're just another living
thing on the surface of the planet, no different to the creatures
and plants around you.

Feel the earth surround you, hold you. It's always there.
Sometimes you can feel buried or stifled, but it can also be a
refuge, a hiding place of safety.

What is your connection to the earth, right now? Nothing
else matters but this. Breathe, feel. Just connect, be part of the
land. Hold it, as it holds you.

When you are ready, return home and eat something solid. Give thanks for the food that was grown in that same earth. Honour your connection to the life around, the life you take in and the life you are living. Every tiny creature plays its part as it grows, feels and explores.

As an alternative option, if you are truly housebound, find a potted plant and touch the earth that holds it. Gently dip your fingers into it, stroke the leaves, petals and stem. Feel the remembrance of deeper lands, as you dream of the outside, but still feel the ground beneath your feet. It doesn't matter if you're reaching through concrete – the Earth is still there, always.

Take the time to stop, feel and connect. Remember who and where you are.

Hiding in Darkness

Happiness can be found, even in the darkest of times, if one only remembers to turn on the light. – Albus Dumbledore

Much of modern spirituality focuses on light. 'Bright blessings', 'may the light shine upon you' ... best intentions.

Too much light is blinding. Being dragged into the light, exposing every tiny aspect of yourself to scrutiny, can be overwhelming. We are animals – sometimes, we need to flee into the darkness, to hide, to heal.

Depression can send us back to our safe places, wherever that may be. A sofa wrapped in a blanket, under a duvet ... a tiny space, just for us.

Find your refuge, but don't be passive. Sit in it. Feel it. Be aware of the space, the protection of

your surroundings, any objects that bring comfort. This isn't about the fear. You are safe here.

Our ancestors sat in caves, in small huts, together or alone. Light was valuable and limited. The darkness around held its own secrets.

Don't let it overwhelm you. Be part of that darkness. You're a creature in it, feeling the safety that it brings, the refuge.

Close your eyes. Reach into yourself. Feel the pain. Let it rise, if you wish. Hold on to your comfort object, keep in contact with the tangible world. You're safe. Darkness within meets darkness without ... both are yours. What do you do with that knowledge?

Breathe deeply. Hold on to your Self, remember who you are. The darkness may wash over you, but you are still part of it, safe, held. Feel it. Remember that you're in your safe place.

Whenever you wish, open your eyes, turn on the light. Remember how the darkness felt. Was it good, bad, or just itself?

Darkness can hold pain, but it can also heal from within its safe unknown. Facing it is more than most people can ever do. Those who realise the power of their relationship with what's hidden behind the light are the bravest of all.

The most problematic depression episodes plunge me into a feeling of disconnection. I am no longer a part of the world. All the colours, meaning and richness become hidden or lost to me. There is a numbing absence of feeling that strips away any inspiration and creativity. I become dead to myself, a husk, a shell. The fall into this state can be violently fast, although the triggers have all been external. Life does not treat many of us kindly.

Most of the time, I draw inspiration from the world around me. That sense of connection to all other living and perhaps-not-living things nourishes and sustains me. Being pushed out of that sense of belonging is brutal. I have self-esteem issues and, subjected as I was to barrages of abuse, bitter criticism, invasive scrutiny and some terrifying processes in my life, I've been crushed, repeatedly. I've come to places where I've felt so awful that the only imaginable way out, I thought, was to die. I'm still alive because of the love and dedication of my husband. I hold the hope that I won't have to crawl through hell again anytime soon, that I can build internal reserves strong enough to resist external pressures.

Love is the most magical and healing force. When it flows to us from others, it restores, uplifts and inspires. On good days, the warmth of the sun and the embrace of darkness feel like manifestations of love because my heart is open. On the bad days, I'm closed, shut down by wounding so that I forget how to give, how to love, and need to be held gently until I can remember again. When you're closed protectively like that, it's also very hard for the good stuff to get in.

*The darkest places, those of most painful experience were reached when I lost my sense of Druidry, or had it ripped from me – when all I could see was the betrayal and cruelty inherent in life. Last time someone put me on my knees, I realised a thing: Justice does not exist. If I want it, I have to **make** it, for myself and others. Fairness, peace, hope … so many things will not be real in the world unless someone makes them. If not me, then who? Perhaps in trying to make these things, I can find some inner peace for myself.*

I don't know if this line of thinking will make any difference next time I'm pushed into the darkness. I do expect there to be a next time, because life is not kind. I just keep hoping that I can handle it better, learning enough to survive the next time and maybe use some of these insights to make things a bit better for others. Depression makes people selfish in its effect, even though it doesn't feel like that when it's happening to you. It's the aftermath of depression that has taught me most about compassion.

Nimue

Body and Land

And forget not that the earth delights to feel your bare feet and the winds long to play with your hair. – Kahlil Gibran

Pagans are often referred to as 'tree-huggers' – with negative connotations, despite the true meanings of this term. Yet many of us have 'favourite' trees, those we see regularly on walks, friends we see change as the year moves in its endless cycle, secret hideaways from childhood.

Sometimes a tree can be your solace, a companion in a way that no other entity can be.

Depending on your personal practice, a relationship with a non-human living entity (flora or fauna) will vary as it would any other human person. You wouldn't just run up to a total stranger and start unloading your problems with a huge hug.

Nor would you with a tree, I suspect. For the main reason that you would feel silly.

But if that tree were familiar, if you knew it and were known *to* it ... how about then?

Dress appropriately and head out into the world. This can be to a favourite location – a grove in the woods, a public park, or just a bit of land hidden away from the main streets. Or you can wander where your feet take you. While it's important to stay safe, roaming can lead you down paths you'd never normally find ... so keep that balance as you explore.

Find a tree. One that's known to you is good, but a friendly-seeming stranger that appeals may be just as appropriate.

Take a look at the tree. Really look. The bark, the leaves, the buds, the colours, the textures. Touch if you feel comfortable. Ask permission (whether verbally or wordlessly) if that helps.

Take a seat if you would like, or simply place a hand on the tree trunk ... and see what starts to flow from within you.

Trees surround us every day, yet it's easy to just miss them, as literally part of the landscape. In this way, we often don't see those human people around us as they pass us by. We don't look, we don't realise. Stranger or friend, we're caught up in ourselves.

When life is hard, that's even more true. Yet a creature of the wild won't judge. It may seem confused as to why you're worrying so much, but it will listen. If you've ever poured your heart out to your dog or cat, you'll know.

Take a deep breath ... and let yourself open. Let your thoughts flow, honestly, no matter how negative or irrational. Cry if you need to. You're not 'dumping' your emotions, you're letting them out. They've been dammed up long enough, the pressure is too tight.

Let the tree bear witness. It's not going to tell you you're stupid or wrong. It hears the wind, the chattering of the birds, the rainfall – you're just another song, pattering around it. Speak if you feel comfortable, or just allow the sounds of your sorrow to come out.

Take a deep breath. Taste the air, the land around. Wet or dry? Hot or cold? You're feeling it. You're not cut off, not alone.

Feel your feet on the floor, your hands touching something solid – be it tree trunk, damp moss or leaf mulch. You're part of this, this world, this place. You're doing what you need to do. Venting, ranting ... healing.

Journeying through my daily walk, I have found that not every day is 'sunshine and butterflies'. Those darker moments, where every-thing in the world seems to get placed into my metaphorical rucksack, can prove to be some of the more difficult times.

I have utilized a lot of techniques and concepts to combat those moments – with mixed results. When I started walking the path of Druidry, I found that meditative states were particularly helpful, but I had trouble achieving focus in the various seated postures. A fellow Druid suggested that I try working through the same meditative techniques, but to do so while walking. This helped me in focus, but I soon found that walking through my neighbourhood was not that safe.

So I started choosing walking trails near me, making each hike into a full-fledged expedition. I found that I started looking forward to each hike, and that spending time out amongst the trees or down by the lake allowed me to set down my rucksack of issues and enjoy the moment for what it was.

Over the past few years, I have come to cherish these particular times, when I can let go of my personal issues and take in the environment around me. Allowing me to set down that rucksack, even for just a little bit, has made all the difference.

Tommy

Journeying

Not all those who wander are lost. – J.R.R. Tolkien

Sometimes, when you're in a dark place, leaving the safety of your home can be a huge step. Heading out into the world is a task akin to climbing Mount Everest. Facing people, unknown circumstances, the sheer weight, noise and madness of Society ...

But that's the goal. What about the *path* to that place of challenge?

Journeys are transitional places, neither here nor there. It may not seem so, but our commute to work, walk to the shops or bus journey into town can be private time, peaceful, just watching the world go by as we move without (too much) conscious effort.

Our feet can take us wherever we wish, after all.

We can grab on to that magical liminality, lose ourselves in it as we observe the faces of others, the wildlife amid the urban landscape, simply letting ourselves ride.

Journeys don't need to be stressful. We can't always get there faster, no matter how much we fret. We don't need to be working while we travel. On public transport, we can disappear into our thoughts, hidden with headphones or sunglasses, but secretly watching. In a car, our minds' pay attention to the driving but we can allow ourselves to be buoyed up by the music of the radio, the scenery, our own little piece of time.

Pause before stepping out of the door, to wherever you have to go. Take a deep breath. Look around, at your home. It'll still be here for you when you get back.

Consider the journey itself. What might you see? What can you observe, as you travel? Just observe, watch, see what there is to see.

Don't worry about what you'll be faced with at the end of the journey – that'll come soon enough. By the time you get

there, you'll be ready for it. Because you'll have experienced the journey, fully, keeping hold of yourself all the way.

But first, just be present, now, you. Breathe deeply. This is *your* time.

When you're ready (or even if you can just catch a moment before your mind starts to panic and draw you back) – step forward. You're moving. Keep going.

The magic of a journey is that ultimately, you can end up wherever you wish. You make your decision, set your intention, and go. Even if it's to a place of challenge, there's a reason why you're going there. Find that, remember it, be resolute. You can leave if you wish.

There will always be places of refuge.

Because sooner or later, there'll be another journey, taking you somewhere else. That time is always there, a tiny escape, but with the potential for so much freedom.

Explore around the next corner. There may be more to see than you think.

Since my late teens I cannot remember life without depression. It took 20 years for me to find the root cause, although I do believe that depression changes with you, making it hard to find a solution.

Despite having a loving family, I felt totally disconnected and alone. I was the strong one who made things happen and kept us all going, as well as helping others on a daily basis in my healthcare work.

Outwardly, I appeared bubbly and happy, but inside I was crying and angry. Sometimes I was furious at everything and just needed space. At other times I was in despair – what was the point in my life? There seemed to be no purpose, no reward, just relentless service to others with nothing for myself. I was raised a Christian, but the beliefs I was pursuing fed my anger without feeling comfortable or true.

*Finally, I realised that my love for Nature was what gave me strength – I'd spent the last 20 years following a Pagan style of life! So, I read more about Druidry, the Gods and Goddesses, and questioned what I **really** thought and felt. Before long, I felt a sense of connection with the 'greater world.' Even though nothing had physically changed, my perception **had.** I was braver about speaking my truth and recognising my needs before helping others.*

*The question in my head of 'What is there for me?' was answered by Nature: 'You have us.' This association feels **so** much more relevant and honest to me, and I have a sense of authenticity in my life now.*

I feel more connected and understand that when I get depressed, it's because I have lost that connection with myself and my truth. I simply walk out into the countryside, sit and watch, listen and be still. I am, at last, treating myself as I have treated others – with kindness and respect.

It's still on-going work, but the Druid path has given me the space to be who I am.

Sara

Long Nights

Always winter, but never Christmas. The Lion, the Witch & the Wardrobe, by C.S. Lewis

Our ancestors understood the importance of darkness. It was something they lived with, sunset to sunrise, with no convenient light-switches to drive the night back. Fire was to be valued, honoured for its warmth, but in the knowledge that the darkness was just a breath of wind away.

There is evidence, in both physical remains and stories, of rituals that honour the dark while celebrating the returning of the light. From barrows in Ireland, situated perfectly to allow the rising sunbeams to enter, to womb-like caverns in Greece, allowing rebirth through personal challenge.

One of the things that darkness makes us do is face our fears. The simple (and yet so complex!) fear *of* the dark and what it holds; the claustrophobia of an enclosed space with no light; the agoraphobia of a totally black landscape, with nothing there but you. It's human nature to want to force these fears away, control them, remove our discomfort. But in Druid practice, facing the fears is essential – to understand, to explore, and ultimately to see the truth of what's really there.

When the darkness has us, when we're in the grip of bleak, isolating terrors within our own minds, it's perhaps easier to relate to those ancestors, alone in their homes. It's not a matter of 'worshipping the sunrise'. It's about not taking for granted that the sunrise is even going to happen. The dark night feels as if it will go on forever, with no respite.

Some psychologists believe that this ancestral memory is the root of depression, that it's part of the 'fight or flight' instinct of our animal DNA. Lost without a place in this technologically advanced modern world ... but a world which, as we all know, still has its fears.

At those times when the night is darkest, those 4 am moments, the sunrise is mere minutes away – and yet it seems a lifetime. People tell you that you'll get through, that it'll be OK, but it's easy to doubt when you feel in your soul that this night will never recede.

Sometimes all you can do is sit. Under a duvet or blanket, a child's safety barrier, but also warmth, comfort. Find your space.

Remember your ancestors. You're not alone. They've all done this before you, sat where you're sitting, doubted, feared.

Not taking that sunrise for granted is an act of faith. Trust that it will happen. This isn't intellectual knowledge ('of *course* the sun will rise!') but soul-deep belief. The magic and joy of that first sunbeam is one of the most powerful sights that we can ever behold – and it happens every day if we let it, if we bear witness.

Trust that the darkness will be driven back, by your own inner fire and will but aided by the brightness outside. Trust that you *will* be able to see it again – in full colour, not just shades of grey.

Our ancestors armed themselves, mentally and physically, against the darkness. Light a candle. Find warm food or drink. A personal charm can help to comfort you, keep you company – from a piece of jewellery given by a loved one, to a battered cuddly toy or worn blanket.

This isn't a time to be thinking about what you *should* be doing. It's what you *need* to do, what you know inside is important. Often that's as simple as stopping, resting, taking stock or considering. Or just sitting, being. That's enough.

If you want to think, reach out for something that inspires you, kindles the flame inside – personal creativity perhaps, a children's book or movie. Let nobody judge you. This is your space.

It may take effort, but when you feel the moment when the

shell around you starts to crack, when the dawn finally comes and the cloud lifts, hold onto that for dear life!

Because that's the memory to keep with you when the night comes again.

I have a shawl that comforts me
I wove each thread, through thick and thin.
I wrap it tightly around me
To hold me safe within.

Cat

Nakedness

Remembering that you are going to die is the best way I know to avoid the trap of thinking you have something to lose. You are already naked. There is no reason not to follow your heart. – Steve Jobs

We talk of stripping ourselves back to basics, baring our souls. But how much harder is it to bear our bodies?

In this modern world of idealised images, physical perfection as depicted on film, many of us are self-conscious of our own forms. Very few are comfortable in their skin; there's always something that we'd like to change.

That's just aesthetically, in terms of image as it appears to others. What about those who cannot change what they physically have to live with? Those with bodily disabilities or 'deformities', which they may or may not be able to hide. These are facts, hard realities of everyday life.

Our bodies limit us somewhat – from having to navigate a world that may not help our abilities, to dealing with those around whose stares pierce more deeply than they should. But our bodies also free us. Without our physical forms, we would not be able to experience the world around, connect with it, feel it with our senses.

How much do we take each of those for granted? A touch, a scent, a taste, a sound, a vision ...

Find an object that you can hold easily in your hand. Natural, organic items are

good – a piece of fruit, a leaf – but it can be anything.

Focus on this object, with all of your senses. Consider each in turn. Touch, look, smell, listen, taste. Explore, be curious.

What did you think when you first picked up the object? What are you thinking now? How much more do you know the object, have a truer understanding of it?

Now, the more difficult challenge.

Find a mirror. Full-length is best, but whatever is available, so that you can see yourself.

Look at yourself. Really look, even if it's difficult. Imagine you're a stranger, seeing yourself for the first time. What is your skin like, your hair, your eyes? What are your clothes saying about you? What story are you telling, right now?

Remove your clothes and look again.

If you have chosen not to do this, ask yourself why. Challenge yourself to do it. It's hard, but it's something that you do every day without thinking about it. Nobody else is there to judge you.

What do you see?

Use your senses. Really focus. Look, touch, listen, taste, smell. Investigate yourself, as you are. You can't change yourself in this moment – this is you. How well do you know yourself?

Yes, there will be areas that you like and dislike. Why is that? Is that your own opinion, or someone else's?

Which areas cause strong emotion, and why? Don't judge – just witness and consider. Learn the story that you body holds, the childhood scrapes, the adult scars. Old injuries, stretch marks, tattoos ... changes that you have made, and changes made to you.

That is all. Get dressed again when you are ready, and step back out into the world.

Take time to look at yourself every now and again. This is you.

The challenge is to know yourself, as you really are. This allows you to better create how others see you, but also to smile when they are clearly blinkered by their own prejudices.

Consider how you view other people, as well. What do their bodies say? How do you think this is interpreted by the world – and by you?

The Blood of the Ancestors

There is no king who has not had a slave among his ancestors, and no slave who has not had a king among his. – Helen Keller

We all carry within us the heritage of our line, the scientific DNA and cosmic spirit of those who've lived before us. From our Mother and Father, to their Parents, to *their* parents, back into the hidden places of history. We have no choice in this – it simply is who we are, the current, living, present representation of our ancestors, the sum total of their learning and experience.

Medical research is beginning to confirm that depression, as a clinical illness, is hereditary. Whether helpful in treatment or not, this also confirms one very important fact: *your ancestors have been where you are.* They went through the same feelings and emotions as you.

They may have stood in very different places to you, through different times. But they looked up at the same stars, considered their own families and friends, worried about their own lives, jobs, children. Humanity hasn't changed that much – what is important is still so, then and now.

This may seem hopeless, then. What's the point, if we're just going to perpetuate suffering through our own biology? And there is no doubt, even if only by law of averages, that some of your ancestors ended their own lives.

The thing to remember is this: your ancestors *lived.* You are here as a clear demonstration of that fact. Children were born, were loved, grew to adulthood and had all of the experiences of their days – resulting in you, now, here. You may be already an ancestor yourself, if you have children of your own. Consider this.

We learn from our ancestors. Speak to them, if you are able. Call or visit those who are still here in person. Work with your

children, when they're having tough times – and when they worry about you. What are you teaching them, what are you passing on with your story and experience?

Those who have passed on can be investigated by genealogical research, archives and records to find names, dates and places. These people were absolutely real. They won't all have been noble, famous or worthy of remembrance. Some will have been bastards, thieves, murderers, or warriors, whores, farmers and housewives. But they all have something to share, if we look.

Set up an altar space to your ancestors, adding things appropriately, to keep them at hand when you need someone to talk to. You may have a keepsake – consider how it was used before it arrived in your hands. Your ancestors were real people too, not just fictitious creations or idealised heroes.

If you are able, meditate or journey to investigate and perhaps communicate directly with those who have passed. This can be challenging, so is best undertaken when you are in a stable enough frame of mind to undertake ritual work.

Visualise your ancestral line reaching out from yourself back into history, and follow it to see who is there. Call upon those who watch over you, ask them to come forward to speak with you. Start close, with those you may have known in life. Use ritual settings which you are comfortable with – these are your relatives, and while they require honour and respect, may not quite understand (or appreciate!) over-flowery language!

Always have food and (non-alcoholic) drink ready for afterwards, to bring yourself back to the present. Grounding is easily forgotten, but working with any form of energy can be taxing, especially when you are not strong in yourself.

While not every one of your ancestors will be sympathetic, understanding or necessarily interested in you, they are all worthy of your time, of honour for lives lived. If they were battling through similar internal feelings to yourself, but in a far harder social situation (and certainly without today's support systems, counselling and medication), how did they do it? What lessons do they have to teach? Why did they make their choices – see things from their point of view.

Human and world history moves forward, constantly, cyclically. There has always been weeping on the field of battle; working before dawn to feed families; hidden pain for the sake of others. But absolutely none of these people were, are or will be alone – their ancestors are with them, surrounding them, waiting and teaching, if we are able to listen.

The Whirlwind

Air

Sometimes, the trick is to keep breathing. – Janice Galloway

Breath is life. Yet we forget it, take it for granted, don't even think about it ... until it's taken away. Stifled, panicking, we gasp for air, throat tight, lungs frozen – until our body remembers the reflexes needed just to stay alive.

Stop moving. Focus. Take a deep breath in, and let it go. Another, through your nose. A third, through your mouth. Steady, controlled. How does that feel? How is each breath different? How does awareness make it different?

Taste the air around as you breathe in through your mouth. Smell it through your nose. Let those sensations touch the back of your throat as the air moves to your lungs ... and feel them fill, expand and contract. Your body knows what to do, but how aware of it are you? Listen, feel, taste, smell.

Touch your breath. Raise your fingers to your mouth and feel it, the warm exhalation, tickling across your skin.

Remember the sensation of panic, the involuntary tightness, brain suddenly flooded with oxygen as you start to gasp or pant. While *remaining fully in control*, breathe a little faster, increasing slowly. Experiment – *you are in control*. Feel how your body changes to compensate, muscles tensing. Your animal self, remembering an ancient instinct – fight or flight?

Let your breath slow again. Slow it even further if you can, breathing out for a count of 5, then in for a count of 5. Pause between breaths. Pause, holding the air inside you.

You are part of this process. You can control it. Fast or slow, your body understands. Hold on to the feelings of the calm breathing. You can return to this whenever you want – simply stop and feel it. Touch it. Remember.

Potential

I only write because there is a voice within me that will not be still.
— Sylvia Plath

Our creativity reflects who we are.

The connection to that wonderful well of inspiration can be blocked, but never severed. The trick is to remember how to find it through the murk.

Visualize your block. Is it a brick wall? Thick black smoke? A tangle of thorns?

Draw it. Taste it.

Face it. Embrace it.

The darkness is yours, part of you. It exists for a purpose. You can run from it, but you can never get away. You can only turn and face it.

Now explore it on your terms. See its potential. Draw out the negative, pin it to a page or spin it into a pattern. Where did it come from? What is it trying to do?

Make it yours. Transform it into something – and allow yourself to be transformed.

Book Divination

Good books don't give up all their secrets at once. – *Stephen King*

Sometimes it takes the smallest thing to distract your mind, engage it and draw it into another, better place.

Find a place with a variety of books. If you don't have your own at home, ask a friend if you can visit to investigate their shelves, or find a local library, charity shop or bookshop.

Let your eyes wander across the spines before you. What are you looking for? Answers? Hope? Direction?

Let your hand pick out a book. Whichever one feels interesting to you. It can be anything, anything at all.

Open it at random. Flick through or let it fall to a well-worn page.

What do you see?

Sometimes the answer is there waiting, in a random sentence of inspiration.

If you're not able to go out, find a favourite book and try this anyway. Many spiritual people use their preferred sacred text, but it works just as well with 'Alice in Wonderland' or 'Sherlock Holmes'.

Imagine the writer, pen to page, ideas flowing. Let yourself be inspired.

Pause

"You just think lovely wonderful thoughts," Peter explained, "and they lift you up in the air." – 'Peter Pan', by J.M. Barrie

Not everyone can face their own Darkness. Some fall, overcome, the journey of life simply too much. The modern malady of Depression, the ancient malaise of melancholy or ennui, can encourage us to give up, to simply sit down on the side of the road and refuse to go further.

Sometimes that pause by the side of the road is needed. We must regroup, marshal our Selves, our resources, strengths and allies.

Find an object that brings you comfort. A photograph, a piece of jewellery. Or a song, a story, a particular taste or scent.

Take time to sit with it. Examine it, with all of your senses. Look at it, touch it, smell it, taste it, listen to it. Get to know it, inside and out. When you close your eyes, know it so well that you can visualise it easily.

You hold that within you. It is yours, whenever you need it. Reach out and touch it again, feel it there with you.

Sensory memory cuts through irrational fear, as we remember safety, better times. If the feeling inspires a smile, it's doing well.

There is always time. Stop yourself, or explain to others around that you need to take a moment. Many people want to, but just can't bring themselves to even slow down. You may inspire others to do the same.

You can find safety, no matter where you are. Look within, at everything you hold dear. It's with you.

*The biggest aid that I've found in dealing with my depression is recognising that it's not always **me** that's the problem. Whether you believe in external spirituality or not, it's important to recognise the outside agents that can be making things worse rather than better.*

*In my case, I recognised wonky neuro-chemistry as that external agent, tricking the 'me' part of my mind, my ego if you like, into believing that there was something wrong. It became quite adversarial: **'me'** – the bits of my personality I wanted to be – against **'it'** – the vicious, twisted bits that tried to make me unhappy.*

*Before that realisation, I had spent months (maybe even years) of ever-deepening desperation, as I listened to **'it'** casting about for reasons behind my unhappiness. I would latch onto anything I could find and ended up variously blaming physical illness, dissatisfaction, even my long-suffering – and awesome – wife for my moods. They were never the problem; it was always the chemistry itself whispering dark thoughts in my ear.*

Sure, there were things that I actually had to address (most pressingly being unhappiness at work) before I could really start to deal with the roots of the problem, but unhappiness at work is a far cry from real depression.

Remember, it's not necessarily your fault. Remember that something may be doing this to you, whether you believe that it's chemistry or something else. Remember that you can't 'snap out of it'; all you can do is put your brain on the 'naughty step' and wait for the tantrum to subside.

And when all else fails, I still fall back on one thought, the vehemence and whimsy of which are central to its power: "Fuck my brain. My brain is an idiot. Don't listen to it."

Matt

Medicine

Always laugh when you can – it is cheap medicine. – George Gordon, Lord Byron

We are fortunate to be living in a time where so-called 'mental illness' is at least recognised as something to be investigated and treated, rather than simply hidden away. Within living memory, asylums were terrifying places, virtual prisons for those considered beyond help but with no other option available.

However, even today it can be difficult to get support from the medical systems that are apparently set up for that purpose. Inner turmoil is, by definition, subjective. An overcrowded health service simply does not always have time to give everyone the attention that they might need. Harassed doctors prescribe pills or add names to a waiting list. The pain continues.

Many people now seek 'alternative' medicine – from crystal healing to homeopathy, shamanic soul retrieval or Reiki. The results may be as varied as any prescribed medication, but we at least have the opportunity to investigate methods to heal ourselves, to work consciously and responsibly within our own experiences. It is important to remember that there is no 'magic bullet' or single 'happy pill' solution – we must retain our judgement as to what is good or bad for ourselves.

In Pagan terms (both ancient and modern), it can be helpful to explore what 'medicine' truly is. Literally, 'the art of healing', medicine can refer to *any* healing method or item *that works*. Depending on what is considered 'normal' by your own society, the shaman's magic bundle is comparative to the familiar Doctor's bag. Sage incense may help you – or simply the smell of good, nourishing food from a warm kitchen.

What 'heals' you? Consider this question.

What makes you feel truly Yourself again? A nice cup of

tea? The company of loved ones? Peace and quiet? A rock concert or football match?

Investigate different forms of medicine *for you:*

Pieces of music, movies or books

Places that you can visit, walk or sit

Company (human or animal)

Artefacts that bring you comfort

A scent or taste that brings you back to yourself

Exercise that raises your heart-rate

Let yourself explore!

If need be, report back to your doctor or counsellor, to enlist their help.

When I was pregnant with my eldest daughter, I spent a lot of time thinking about Mother Goddesses and what kind of Mum I would become. I lit lots of candles and offered lots of mead. Then I got pre-eclampsia and my girl was delivered at 32 weeks by caesarean. After I recovered from the operation I was sent home, and she stayed in hospital for the full eight weeks until her due date.

I was so angry at the world, and so depressed. I stopped doing anything spiritual; I lit no incense, I couldn't meditate. Although I knew about the risks of pregnancy from books, I had never believed they would happen to me – that rocked my belief in absolutely everything.

I had to change my definitions of what a mother is and does into something that I didn't recognise. There's no template for a SCBU mum – it's too modern, clinical, unnatural. It just didn't fit with all the things I had planned.

Two years later I was pregnant again, and again got pre-eclampsia, but much more dramatically. My second little lady was born at 29 weeks and very poorly; we were told to prepare for the worst. While it was probably the darkest moment I have had so far, it was also one of the most spiritual.

In my morphine-induced haze, I could see many women standing before me, with me. All these generations of mothers standing side by side, who had all faced the very real possibility that they would lose their babies. All these women knew the depth of that pain, just standing there, just with me. I think I felt more connected to my ancestors in that moment than at any other.

When I finally got home, I dusted off my candles and lit them for those women. They all walked with me through the long four months until my daughter was allowed home. My grandmothers.

I am very lucky – both my little girls survived. I had spent so long looking to myths and legends for spiritual awareness, it was right there all along, in my own ancestors.

Jo

False Smiles

Just because I'm smiling, doesn't mean I'm happy. – Unknown

Inside, I'm screaming, but no one can hear me. Outside, I look the same as you. – Adele

Many depressed people learn very quickly how to act. How to fake it, keep a smile on your face, go through the motions, get by. Work needs to be done, family relationships need to be maintained. By keeping the mask firmly in place, we can maintain the illusion, go about our business.

We know full well that it's not true. That we're just hiding. Often because we don't know what else to do. The thought of doctors, medication, institutionalisation ... and social stigma, possible loss of job, loved ones. What will people *think*?

What do *you* think?

I'm not suggesting that we all take our masks off and throw them away (although that would be good). That's not always possible. But depending on how much Paganism you've read about or experienced, you may have encountered the spiritual idea of masks, rather than psychological.

Like children, we can make masks. Clay, plaster, special effects equipment. Ready-made masks are easy to find, but can then be customised – feathers, beads, wood, leaves. It can feel silly, but it's an interesting exercise: to give form to your own mask. Is it beautiful or monstrous? Is this smile genuine or a fixed rictus grin?

You can make your mask, physically, to explore why it's there. Or you can simply visualise it.

Take a mirror. Look at yourself. Yes, this is far harder than it may seem at first. Force yourself to look.

What do you see?

If tears fall, let them. But keep looking.

What do you see?

What do you think others see? What do you show them? Smile, as you would for a family member, your boss, a stranger on a train.

Now smile as you would for someone who loves you, genuinely, and that you love in turn. A partner. A child. A pet.

Feel the difference. See the difference. It's not all about your mouth. Look into your own eyes.

See the truth of your smile. Feel the difference between that, and the falseness of the mask.

This isn't about realizing your inner beauty, although that is there. It's about feeling the difference, knowing when it's you, and when you're faking. Because sometimes we forget; the line blurs, and we lose ourselves.

Hold on to your Self. Whenever you look in the mirror, for vanity, make-up or just to brush your teeth. Look into your eyes and see your Self.

Did you ever look into the mirror as a child and try to imagine yourself as a grown-up? See that child, still looking. Sometimes this will help to understand the madness of the adult world – where the mask is a survival tactic, a tool for playing in the insanity around you. And when it needs to be taken off.

With a little practice, you'll soon be seeing the masks of others.

Think of a true friend, that you know well. How do you feel when they're clearly faking themselves, not being 'real' for the sake of image or perceived role?

Speak to the mask. Then speak to the real person. Feel the difference.

Storms

Life isn't about waiting for the storm to pass ...It's about learning to dance in the rain. – Vivian Greene

Screaming at the sky, howling at the moon, dancing in a rainstorm – sometimes yelling into a world is one of the most necessary things you can do to reclaim your sanity.

Civilised we may consider ourselves, but we're still part of this vast and varied planet. Only a tiny step away from the outside, the wild ... the mad.

Consider the difference in elements. The quietness of snow; the power of lightning. Seasonal perhaps, but weather is about as random as can be, viewed from the point of view of a tiny individual on one scrap of land, unable to see the bigger currents and movements except as swirls interpreted for us from a weather map.

When you know that a storm is coming, harness that, connect with it. Even if you feel that you personally have no energy, if you can't get outside ... just open a window and listen.

Feel the storm, the freedom, the flow within it. Currents of wind, gusting clouds, sheets of rain, soaked earth. And you. Not fighting it – part of it.

The Raging Fire

Fire

Do one thing every day that scares you. – Eleanor Roosevelt

You are alive. A warm, moving creature, fuelled by nourishing food and inspiring ideas.

Without the fires of life, you stop. Language reflects this – if we aren't alive, we are frozen, cold, dead.

So when we are unable to move, in the dark, rigid, muscles locked, heart buried deep, stomach taut, how do we restoke our inner fires to move again, to remind ourselves of what being alive feels like?

Sometimes it can seem impossible. We reach out to touch the fire and burn ourselves, just to feel something. We've become distant, removed, almost un-alive, just going through the motions.

Consider your blood, as it flows through you. Sometimes it helps to see that flow over skin, to remind yourself that your heart is still pumping – but this isn't truly necessary.

Listen. Touch your wrist or throat. Feel your heart. See the colour in your veins. The blood is there, working to maintain life, health, movement.

Consider your mind. You're thinking right now, as these little word-shapes enter your eyes and transform into ideas. What are you thinking? Physical circuits fire as you ponder, generating new thoughts, new ideas. You may be inspired; you may want to turn away.

No matter what, you are still alive. The fire burns within you, heating muscle and skin, organs and bone ... and brain.

Our ancestors believed in the 'fire in the head', the bardic flame that ignites with a shock of inspiration. A single idea that burns inside, pushing you to act, to move, to create.

We all have this inside us. We are all capable of it.

You're creating ideas right now. You can move and do – even the simple act of making a cup of tea, some food, finding a book or TV show to watch. Each of those acts, in turn, keeps you alive physically and distracted and stimulated mentally.

The key is becoming aware of that fire, that flow, that energy. What can you do with it? If you can make tea (in the way that you like, rather than badly), then you can make other things. If you can write down your thoughts on a page, you can read them back and see what other ideas come from them.

Nobody will judge you for these simple acts of creativity. They're purely yours, by and for you. Made with your inner fire. The thing that's keeping you alive – your will, intention, awareness.

It may feel like it's gone or buried, but it will always be there, so long as you are thinking.

Wildness at Work

When you're lost in those woods, it sometimes takes you a while to realize that you are lost. For the longest time, you can convince yourself that you've just wandered off the path, that you'll find your way back to the trailhead any moment now. Then night falls again and again, and you still have no idea where you are, and it's time to admit that you have bewildered yourself so far off the path that you don't even know from which direction the sun rises anymore. –
Elizabeth Gilbert

In the ancient tales of Briton, Merlin – that most famous of magicians, bards and (perhaps) Druids – became overwhelmed with the tasks he was facing ... and went mad. He retreated to the forests, walking among the trees and animals, clothes torn, filthy and ragged. Eyes once wide with power and knowledge were now filled with the wildness of the woods. Civilisation was forgotten.

Sometimes we need to step out of the everyday world. We want to retreat to the woodlands, find peace in Nature. Scream into the wild with our own song. It helps.

But this isn't always possible. Our workplace can be a battle-field, our home life full of sound and fury. We feel trapped in our duties, our commitments.

Find a quiet place, just for a few minutes. A bathroom is good, somewhere that you can shut a door and be safe. A peaceful place outside is a true blessing, if there's a small garden nearby.

Take deep breaths. Let the tears flow if need be. This moment is yours.

Remember when you were a child and made up stories, drew pictures, created fantasy.

See the busy world around you as a wild woodland.

Columns and walls are trees, light bulbs – hanging fruit. Desks are thickets, sofas fallen logs. Carpets are leaves, bracken. The noise of ringing phones, raised voices, children yelling – a magpie's chatter, the bark of a wolf, stags locking horns.

We create our own wildness. We try to impose order onto it, but the noise, the clutter, the chaos is all as animalistic and basic as any jungle.

Your spirituality is part of that. Your life is part of that. You are a wild thing, caged – except *you have found a key*. You can open your eyes and truly see the world around. You can laugh at the screaming parrots, the gossiping monkeys, the placid cows. But you understand your relationship to them, as fellow creatures of the world (even if their motivations are a mystery). We're all trying to find our place in this zoo.

You have walked the wild paths, and you will continue to do so – on your own terms. You carry the magic within you. Your ancestors and Gods walk with you. Do you really think concrete and brick can keep them out?

Take a deep breath and head back. Walk in the knowledge of your wild self. Nobody can take that away from you.

Music

You are what you do, not what you say you'll do. – C.J. Jung

Give yourself permission to be creative. Nobody will judge you. Sometimes the best way to express yourself is in that connection with Awen, inspiration. Yes, you can create beauty for others, but sometimes it's more about showing what's inside you, trying to get out – which may not be beautiful at all, but which still needs to be heard or seen.

Find a piece of paper, a sketchpad or journal, and some pens or pencils.

Turn on the radio or music player. A random or favourite station, it doesn't matter. Find a song. Do you love it or hate it? Can you bear it right now? Listen anyway.

Now write, draw or however suits you best, tell the story that you hear in the music. It can be something in the lyrics, or images that spring to mind from an orchestral piece. Go beyond the human voice – hear the instruments, the orchestra, the electronic sounds.

Show the story of the song. Let your mind open to the music as it rises and falls. Find your connection to that short piece.

Play it again if you can; or just remember it in your head. Explore it. Is it deep and profound, or silly and frivolous? Happy dance music or painful death metal? Mozart or Handel, Elvis or Dolly Parton?

Consider what you've created. You can laugh if you want – it probably won't be something to put on show. But you've connected with that song, for that brief moment. With all those who created that ... and you've made something yourself.

What does your own creativity say about you, right now? The key here is exploration, letting your ideas roam when caught in the tunes of others. Your inspiration is entirely unique.

Try to keep what you've made, if you can. Try this exercise again and consider each work in the future, to see what they say. Do they reflect your life, your state of mind, each time? Or is it just scribbling?

Finding connection with the wider world in a (roughly) four-minute song. Not world-changing, but a moment when you've made something that's purely yours.

Dark Stories

Myths are public dreams, dreams are private myths. – Joseph Campbell

Every mythological system has its own interpretation of the journey through inner Darkness. Whether it's Persephone spending six months in the Underworld to reflect Winter, or Inanna willingly questing there to gain knowledge for herself and others, each story has a point.

Some are much more 'human' tales, such as Rhiannon's terrible suffering for truth against deception over the loss of her child. While Cerridwen worked deep magic in her cauldron, her goal was ultimately to help her own son – as any mother would.

A great and immortal deity is not immune to pain or suffering, no matter what their powers may be. Our ancestors who told the tales understood the reality of life – that darkness is part of it, but that we are to explore it, journey through it, battle with it (not always to win), and discover the secrets that it has to tell us.

Of course, that's easy to say. These might seem trivial, fairy-tales, of no help at all to your own situation. Look deeper. These are guiding paths, directions pointing the way forward. Maps can be contained within story as well as moral lessons.

As Pagans, our understanding of deity can be varied, but generally speaking, we are aware of them as real. Whether they are energy forms, actual entities, representations of human arche-types ... it doesn't matter. Consider how you feel about the Gods and Goddesses. Consider how their tales are as valid as those told anywhere else (including in this book). What lessons are they trying to teach?

Consider a mythological tale that resonates with you, sings in your heart, that you love to hear or read again and again. Is this story part of your own ancestral history, the people of your

land? Or has it been brought to you by travellers, bards, voices down the ages?

We may be in the twenty-first century in our 'real lives', but we are still very human – a much older heritage. What was the original objective of this story, do you know? Are you able to find out its history, listen for the thoughts of the author so long ago?

And what is that story telling you *now*? You may not necessarily see yourself as the hero; which character do you feel particular sympathy for, understanding and empathy? Do you know why?

Imagine yourself *in* the tale. At the start is good, beginning the journey, but able to make your own decisions on the path to the conclusion. What would you do in those circumstances? Do you understand the battles that must be fought, the suffering that must be undertaken, to reach that end? Do you learn as the characters learn?

Alternatively, are you looking more into those who evolve differently within the text – those whose ending we *don't* see, who remain in the darkness, who escape or vanish? Where does the 'villain' go – and are they truly evil, or just an instigator, one who challenges? Efnisyen, Loki, Blodeuwedd, Medea ... Where are they, what happens to them?

Each person has their own journey, motivation, reasons for their actions – which are not always simple or easy to understand. Explore those that call to you within the story, see where their paths lead. Feel where your own journey intersects and then moves away again, as you step back into your own life.

What have you learned from the story, from within?

We learn of the different types of darkness – sorrow, anger, revenge, hopelessness. Some offer comfort, others teachings, how to fight, when you need a firm kick in your rear end ... the Gods have been where we are, but while it may appear to be on a much grander scale, the fundamentals are the same. Tears, pain, grief, guilt. Human life lessons.

Pain

Sometimes...you can cry until there's nothing wet in you. You can scream and curse to where your throat rebels and ruptures. You can pray, all you want, to whatever god you think will listen. And, still it makes no difference. It goes on, with no sign as to when it might release you. And you know that if it ever did relent ... it would not be because it cared. – Jhonen Vasquez

Sometimes, the sorrow and hurt inside us transforms itself into pain. Sharp, cutting, demanding to be manifested. Whether harming ourselves or taking the pain out on others – by arguing, yelling, beating at walls, or smashing objects nearby – that scream demands to be released.

Stop, just for a moment – STOP. You're in the eye of the storm.

Feel the pain. Reach into it, go deep. What does it feel like? What does it want? What do you want to do to express it?

See the pain as energy. Is it a fire, raging through your veins? Whitewater rapids? A tornado in your mind? An immense rock in your belly?

How must it come out? How will this volcano erupt?

Grab it, if you can. It's not easy. See yourself taking that pain and riding it. It has to come out somehow, so what are you doing with it? *You?* It's yours. Connect with it, take control of it.

If you're alone, then scream. Cry. Gasp. Do it. Give voice to the emotion. Remember, this is your own sound, not to be shared (and others may try to stop you).

Turn it into song. Find music and join yourself with the flow of another's noise/melody as they let it out into a microphone. Headbang, thrash, express it. You don't need words.

Grab colours and paper – paint. Let the rage express itself, the sorrow bloom. It doesn't matter what it looks like, this is

purely yours. Let your body join with the pen or brush, fling arms as much as you need to. Fingerpaint if you want!

If you're able to, describe it in writing. Trace the words on the page.

If you feel the call to cut, consider your skin, the flow of blood beneath, the tiny cells. Leave the razor – keep hold of the pen or brush, and trace those lines of life. You can wash the ink away, but your body will remain. You're making your own tattoos, with as much care as any needle. The challenge is NOT to pierce the skin, to flow without ripping the canvas. What does the design look like? What have you created? Is it beautiful or hideous? Does it matter?

Take control, harness the emotion.

Breathe. Feel it – fast or slow, calm or hyper? Take one strong deep breath out, let it *whoosh* from your lungs, then suck it back in. A silent scream, shoving oxygen around your bloodstream, into your mind ... and out again. Feel the clean air coming in. What colour is it? What colour is the breath you're sending out? Let it go.

When you feel the storm starting to pass, when the numbness begins to take hold, find a safe place to sit and let the final aftershocks come. Wrap yourself in a blanket, find a hot drink if you are able to. The so very normal routine of making tea can help to focus your mind like nothing else.

Keep breathing. The pressure has been let out. It may return, but it's temporary – and you're still here.

Depression is emotional pain physicalised. For me, my self-harm is chronic. The release is when you actually feel pain (I don't always feel the cuts I made) and that's a difficult thing to replicate. I've tried an elastic band on my wrist – pulling it back and letting go. Holding an ice cube is another option. Neither really worked for me. Then there's the entrancing effect (this is the closest I come to mysticism or spirituality) of seeing the blood pour down my arm and make pools on the floor. That's when the red pen can come into play.

For people like me, self harm isn't an option, it's almost a necessity. The deeper the depression, the less I 'feel'. I do agree that having a creative outlet is a real survival tool.

I've never cut myself with thoughts to kill myself, believe it or not. Depression just makes me incredibly numb.

Ian

I'm not a chronic self-harmer, but I have needed that release. It's not always cutting, but can be hitting or pressure. It tends to happen when I feel numb or overwhelmed and need an anchor. It's like being a ship undergoing tempestuous storms and deathly stillness, trying to find a safe port. There's other self-harming too, such as hair pulling/twisting and picking at your face (I have done both the latter to extremes).

Oddly, running water helps me to centre myself sometimes, as it puts me into a trance and helps me to focus. Painting with my hands can help too, with thick acrylic for the texture. Making dough has a similar effect. I walk barefoot in mud or sand, to feel the sensation. It releases the pressure inside.

It's not failing if you do self harm, even if you try alternatives, but it may indicate that you need to talk to someone – clearly, what you are experiencing is getting too much. Often it's not about death or ending it, just about finding something to hold on to.

Emma

Suicide

In the end, one needs more courage to live than to kill himself.
– Albert Camus

Suicide is still one of the greatest mysteries and taboos within our society. Even though it is the cause of so many deaths every year, it still baffles many of those who remain.

I can only talk about this from my own experience. Do not feel obliged to read this chapter if you are not able. But if you do read on, I ask you to consider these words together with me.

I was once asked by a workmate what it actually felt like to be 'depressed'. I described some of the feelings that I have when I'm in the low places – and her face changed utterly. The sheer amazement and shock, as she stammered that she had never realised it was possible to feel such things. Her father was on anti-depressant medication at that time, and she hadn't been sure how to deal with him – with the half-felt thought that it was 'all in his head'.

On one hand, I envy those who have apparently never felt such things. On the other, I doubt that they are really being honest with themselves. We've all thought about what it would be like if we were no longer here; from that first time when, as children, we realise that we are finite entities, with limited time on Earth.

Considering mortality is entirely natural. If you don't, it can come as an even greater shock when you are faced with it, when you are inevitably forced to face the reality of imminent death (be it your own or someone close to you). Humanity is a condition with a 100 per cent mortality rate, after all.

Sometimes, when the darkness surrounds you, it's impossible to escape the very real possibility of Not Being Here. The idea that it might actually help: the pain may stop, others may benefit, and suchlike. But when actually challenged, we see that these ideas are irrational, not based on truth. They are a challenge to ourselves to be overcome, to prove that we want to live, and are worthy of being alive.

In the past, medical professionals have asked me (as part of the form-filling part of their role) whether I have considered suicide. When I answer 'Yes', they look up at me. Have I ever made plans – prepared a Will, set my affairs in order? 'No.'

I explain to them that the moments of passionate doubt come upon me so strongly that it's not a question of preparation. My urges have been more impulsive, in the moment – the wrench of the

wheel while driving to take me off the road; the time spent in the
kitchen considering pill bottles; the purchase of razor blades that
remained in their packet, unopened.

The fact that I can rationally talk about it seems to confuse.

Death is deeply personal. I don't understand how it can be considered 'cowardly' – it can be the bravest thing that a person can do in their situation. Those who have actively faced it are, in my experience, some of the most thoughtful people that I have met.

Questions, then: is the act of suicide really true and honourable, for me? Can I rise to the challenge of simply staying alive?

When faced with thoughts that the world may be better without me in it, challenge those words. Visualise them, imagine them being said by someone else – and allow yourself the power to answer.

- **Consider the things that you have accomplished, and those that you have yet to do. You have got this far.**
- **Think of your dreams, the experiences that you still haven't had but would yet like to explore.**
- **Yes, remember loved ones. You know that you would be missed.**
- **Call to mind a time of great pleasure and enjoyment, when you were truly able to laugh, love, be yourself. You can seek that out again.**

These are the challenges to the words that come from the dark places. I am sure you can think of more – what is truly important to you? Search deeply, look inside. Find and hold on to your Self, the Me that sits lost and uncertain in the eye of the storm.

What do *you* want to do, really? No obligation, guilt or

direction from another. YOU.

So now, do something. Write, draw, play a game, go for a run – use your mind, focus your thoughts and hands, direct yourself to *do*. While you are doing, you are still moving forward, still actively being yourself. Living.

Live honourably. Make your life the best that it can be, for you. This is not a matter of pressure or expectation – just simply being there to witness the sunrise tomorrow can be enough.

To live will be an awfully big adventure. – Peter Pan

2008-9 were meant to be great years for me. I was the Deputy Lord Mayor of my city, looking forward to becoming Lord Mayor. I was a successful Councillor, with a well-paid job, a nice car and home, and a lovely family.

Then things changed. Not straight away, but gradually, slowly, often unnoticed by anyone – including me. I started feeling pressured and found it hard to cope with the things I was used to doing. My Council work started to suffer. When I went to meetings, I would often slip out part way through and walk around for a while, or worst still, just go home.

I was soon spiralling out of control and still didn't realise it. I was constantly snapping at my wife and kids, or would just walk out of the house, making excuses for my behaviour. Then I found a small bedsit and moved out, leaving my family shattered.

I hit rock bottom. Car, job, home, girlfriend, dreams all lost in a week.

I wanted to end it all on a Saturday night. I got drunk on a bottle of whiskey and took the kitchen knife to my wrist. With tears streaming down my face, I was about to sink the blade into my flesh, when, for no reason, I turned around and looked directly at a photo of my two youngest children smiling at me. I couldn't do it to them. I had ruined their lives by walking out on them; I couldn't leave them without their Dad as well. I put the knife down, and cried uncontrollably for a few hours. I then made plans to get my life back on track.

I fought the depression over the next few months – and won.

From the darkness I was in, my children – without knowing it – became the light to lead me out of my despair. Whilst their Mum has moved on with her life, I love my children more now than I have ever done.

Sometimes, your light of inspiration is right in front of you, but it won't shine for you until it's the right time. Then when it does, you wonder why you ever could have taken that light for granted.

Rob

Passion and Focus

Passion. It lies in all of us. Sleeping ... waiting ... and though unwanted, unbidden, it will stir ... open its jaws and howl. It speaks to us ... guides us. Passion rules us all. And we obey. What other choice do we have? Passion is the source of our finest moments. The joy of love ... the clarity of hatred ... the ecstasy of grief. It hurts sometimes more than we can bear. If we could live without passion, maybe we'd know some kind of peace. But we would be hollow. Empty rooms, shuttered and dank. Without passion, we'd be truly dead. – Joss Whedon

We're not really encouraged to fight these days – unless you're employed and trained specifically for that purpose. Instead, the 'Keep Calm and Carry On' mentality prevails. Carry on regardless, battle through, stiff upper lip and all that ...

Sometimes, though, fighting helps. The anger, frustration and sheer pent-up emotion won't stay quietly buried. We want to lash out, often at those who simply had the bad luck to be in our way at the wrong time.

Fighting doesn't necessarily mean reflexive rage, either. Skilful soldiers and athletes aren't foolish or ignorant. Consider some of the great fighters of legend. Gods of war who were also cunning tacticians. Warrior women with hearts full of moral courage and intelligence.

We learn from our stories. The reason that they are still told is because they are still relevant – the 'good' ones and the 'bad'.

Odin hung from the World Tree for nine days and nights to acquire knowledge. He became intimately acquainted with pain, starvation and thirst, sacrificing an eye so that he could see more deeply. He is both warrior and storyteller, traveller and teacher.

Athena burst from the head of Zeus fully grown, clad in armour and ready for battle. Yet her totem is the owl, bird of wild wisdom. Athens, the city that took her name, was famous for its military might and as a centre of learning.

Fitness and sports instructors know all about the enthusiasm that new students exhibit when keen to show off in a first lesson. But their random flailing is evidence of nothing except passion – which is all very well, but without training and focus, can easily be beaten ... or take over.

Do you choose your fights well, or lash out? Does the rage and frustration inside rule you? After an argument, do you feel satisfied or just regretful? Who do you want to fight – others or yourself?

Consider the reasons for a confrontation. In your heart, do you truly believe it? Or is this simply pent-up emotion, self-hatred or frustration at your own lack of ability to control or change a situation?

Consider the weapons that you may have at hand. Your own skills, knowledge, allies. How may they best be deployed?

Consider your goal. What do you hope to achieve from a battle? Is it really worth it? Sometimes true bravery comes from walking away with your integrity intact.

Passion comes from deep, heartfelt feeling about an issue. When something matters that much, for a deeply held and true reason, it is often worth fighting for.

But whether it is for love, honour or some other deeply held personal belief, knowing the truth within yourself is the first step. Otherwise the fight will continue, again and again, long after you are beaten.

The Rushing Torrent

Water

Water does not resist. Water flows. – Margaret Atwood

Our bodies may feel solid, but so much of them are water. Our brain floats inside our skull.

We're told that it's unacceptable to let ourselves 'leak' through excess emotion or lack of control – from crying to drooling, bleeding to pissing. Yet all of these are entirely natural acts, and often involuntary.

How do we connect to our own flows? Women have their menstrual cycle, but we're all part of the gravitational pull of the planet, subject to the ebb and flow of the tides. We all have our own ups and downs, no matter how severe or shallow.

How do you feel *right now*? Broad descriptions – up or down, happy or sad? Now deeper – tired, confused, hyper, chaotic.

Pick one of those words, the one that seems to best match your current state of mind. Focus on that single word. What does it mean? What images does it conjure up? Why does it apply to you so well, right now?

Where will that emotion take you? You can't be tired/confused/hyper/chaotic forever. You might not know what will come next, but something will. Imagine it. Pick your favourite, or perhaps the most likely. Don't judge, try to be realistic (as best you can).

Flow with the words, one after another. Consider the emotions *as words*. Yes, they may feel all-encompassing to you, mind, body and soul, but they are also simply words, just describing (no matter how badly) *you, right now*.

When you feel ready, choose a different word. Calm. Peaceful. Prepared. Myself. Then put that word on, try it for size. See how the emotions of that feel, and if you can find a fit

that suits you.

This isn't trying to force happiness into a sad mind. This is suggesting that the words can help to direct you. You are going with the flow – now add your own oar to that, directing things a little. You might still be drawn with the current, but that's ok. You're still there, a thinking, feeling person. You might not be able to control everything that's going on within (and outside) you, but that flow continues – and you are part of it.

When you are able, give yourself up to the flow of emotion. Let the tears come, if they must. Sooner or later, the flood may reach a waterfall – but that can be ridden, if you are strong enough. It may become calm, but the numb feeling of *be*calmed, unable to go anywhere, dammed, blocked. Let yourself float in that, until you're ready to move forward again.

Hold on to your Self, your mental life raft that is you, your core, the person reading this, considering it right now. The flow is part of you, and you are part of it. Sometimes all it takes it learning how to steer.

Growing up in rural England, my family moved with the turning year, feeling a casually conscious connection to the rhythms that surrounded us every day, creating a very grounded environment in which to grow.

After university, I moved to London where I developed and flourished as a person, socially as a Gay Man and spiritually as a Pagan. As a solitary I'm comfortable in the City, thinking of myself as a 'Pavement Witch', with my sexuality and spirituality being keystones to my everyday experience. I've come to recognise that the City has seasons and rhythms no less than any part of the wild. Seeing these markers of change and stability in the City as the cycle turns has supported and grounded me in the same way as my childhood.

The death of my Mum when I was young left me with a tendency toward depressive episodes. While generally more acute and transient than long-term, mine can be incapacitating: aching, gasping voids with howling winds of utter aloneness and absence. Introspection can be a wonderful and terrible gift, and these storms have been my companions for thirty years. I know them now and have discovered ways that allow me to ride them, even learning a little during the rides.

There comes a point during a storm where I lose control of the dark thoughts in my mind, which can turn toward ending my life. These thoughts used to scare me deeply, but now I've come to recognise them as simply 'false-thinking'. Early in my experience of them I knew that the only safe thing to do was be still, and I'd do this for hours, in fear and anguish; often curled in a ball, not knowing if it would pass. It always has.

Now when darkness descends, I hold a medicine bag that I've made: four stones representing the elements plus one for chaos/storm, two stones for The Lord and Lady respectively, one stone for me, and five dice for life's chances, all tied up in a small leather bag. I guess I'm using these as rosaries or worry-beads. Holding the bag I can feel the contents, and actively recognising each by touch, my mind focuses away from my internal pain, toward contemplation of divinity in all things, of the possibility of change, of the elements of the world around me.

While this hasn't changed the nature of my storms, I'm now able to continue to function, to distinguish (mostly) between the real distress in my mind/heart, and the real normality and joy in the rest of the world. Accepting the first and recognising the second, I can usually interact with people around me in a way that's congruent with both my pain and their joy. If I really can't cope any more, I sit quietly, holding my medicine bag (perhaps hidden within a pocket if I'm out and about), taking a moment to contemplate and ground myself again.

Recently I needed to take a course of treatment for a year, the side effects of which included exhaustion and depression; there have even been suicides. I was worried, but decided to continue, knowing that I'd need support. I began to make preparations – the first of which was to acquire a stick.

A stick could be about sickness and distrust of my body; a cane or short-staff could be about support and an additional connection to the pavements of the City I so love. After selecting a cane, with advice from a member of the oldest cane-making family in London, I began preparations. For a few minutes every day, I meditated on my cane and how it would become part of me, providing an additional connection to the ground I walked on for that year to come. I did this as I would any item that I intended to have particular purpose in my life; is this WitchCraft, or psychology? I don't know if there's actually much of a difference here.

Eventually my first day of treatment arrived, and my first day of taking my cane out with me. We felt strange together! I didn't really need the cane at first, but that was the deal – we were together for a year. So we got to know the roads together, learning a new way of being in the world and a new way of connecting to those spirits of the land.

I came to recognise the spirit of the Hill I live on. This one felt *strong, a little like a Grumpy Old Man, but willing to lend a hand so long as I 'did some of the buggerin' work myself.' I'd ask for a little of his strength in the morning as I walked down the hill, and he'd welcome me off the bus at night, encouraging me to climb his body to my home and rest.*

I also came to recognise the serpent-spirits of the roads where I had most trouble: the paving-slabs and tarmacadam, the scales of their backs. They're beautiful, though often scarred and battered, but still lithe; connecting the City together, paths where countless thousands have passed, leaving a small mark. As I came to know and address them, speaking to them on my seemingly long walks home after work, the pains that developed in my feet as treatment went on were eased. I never felt an answer other than that, but the softening of the pavements and the support I felt flowing through my cane felt real enough to help me home.

While in Town, sitting on a bench during breaks from work (with my cane planted on the ground, connected) I could focus on seeking the energies of the City. I could let the anxiety, exhaustion and negative thoughts subside for a while, and recognise that my City was still a beautiful place, that all this was still there for me when I was able to come back to it. It is this awareness of my surroundings that helps me through my tough times: seeing the cycles, knowing they're still there, still turning.

Steve

Chaos

Panic is ultimate Chaos. Primal brain recalls what it's like to be a cornered animal, and you freeze physically, while your mind goes into overdrive, running in circles, trying to find the way out ... while at the same time, achieving nothing except making the situation worse.

It can be impossible to focus at such times. Slowing your breathing? Meditating? Not always possible.

Taking back control, somehow, is key. And not in a power-over way – but reclaiming yourself, dredging your true thoughts up from the morass of manic, the quiet voice that's you, looking in from outside to say 'what on earth is going on? I don't like this!'

This is a very subjective experience, however. I don't know what calms you. But I can encourage you to explore, to find out.

Find somewhere safe, where you won't be interrupted for a while. This is your own space. There are no immediate threats – you are safe.

Recall how you feel when the panic is rising. That terrible time when it's just *there* inside, present, rising within. You know it's coming, and that makes it worse. You can't escape. Slow or fast, here it comes ...

Call to mind what that feels like, without letting it affect you. What are the physical symptoms? Do your palms sweat? Do you breathe faster? And the mental effects: how far can you concentrate on anything – even just getting away?

Now remember how your thoughts are when the panic is in control. Short, staccato words, maybe: 'no, God, help, escape.' Or negative thoughts, endorsed by whatever's going on around: 'they hate me, I'm useless, what's the point.'

Remember that you are outside this, right now. You're safe. This might take more than one attempt, but you're still in

control of yourself – the panic isn't winning right now.

And how do you feel afterwards? Exhausted, drained, unable to do anything as the panic has stolen your energy, your motivation? Do you want to recover and get on, or just sleep?

Do *not* be judgemental here. None of this is 'bad' (or 'good') – it just *is*. These are your 'symptoms'. Get to know them, and you can work on changing their effect on you.

The trick next is to realise how best to deal with the panic. Earlier is better, when you feel it approaching, but sometimes BAM – there it is. What can you do?

A Buddhist trick is to let the panic wash over you. Remove your Self, your inner thoughts, from the madness and just observe. 'Oh yes, negative thoughts.' This can, however, be difficult, when all you want to do is scream.

Find a safe place and let it run its course. This can be tricky, as you may be in a public place at a bad time (very likely, in fact). But by observing how the panic is when it's not present (as above), you can try to get a sense of your Self – your True Self – as an inner 'safe place', that's always there, like a life-raft to hang on to.

Hold on to your motivation. Remember how awful the panic is – it's not pleasant or enjoyable, or something to be desired. You want your Self back ... so hold on to that feeling. Use a small tool as a reminder, if it helps: a mantra to be chanted quietly, a piece of jewellery to hold as a talisman.

By observing, remembering, objectively witnessing the madness, you can try different tactics to deal with it when it arises. Avoiding it with pills is one, but that may not work forever (or the side-effects may be equally unbearable).

Consider the Celtic knot at the beginning of this chapter. It spins, turns in on itself, appearing chaotic but with a hidden pattern in its depths. One single line, moving in and out. Hold on to that – your Self. The panic may obscure its pattern, but you are still there, moving on in your story. What appears to be

a knot may hold great beauty when observed from outside.

What is the reason for the panic? And how far is that true, valid, something that you want to accept? This knot may be unravelled with a single tug – it's knowing the difference between the chaotic noise and your own song.

Loneliness

When you're surrounded by all these people, it can be lonelier than when you're by yourself. You can be in a huge crowd, but if you don't feel like you can trust anyone or talk to anybody, you feel like you're really alone. – Fiona Apple

Sometimes, it's just you.

This can be pleasant, needed, calmness and peace after chaos and noise. Time for yourself, just to breathe, just to be. Solitary and alone, in your own space.

Or it can be the paradoxical loneliness that you might feel in the middle of a crowd. Claustrophobia, panic or hyper-awareness from the lack of direction. Feeling trapped; the pressure to *do something*, be as expected, act a certain way, it's all just too much ...

When physically alone, you might just feel lost, floating, not knowing what to do. Do you want to break that feeling by calling a friend, allowing someone else to visit – or would that make things worse? Would that take you into the 'public' situation, in which you can't tell anyone how you feel, because you feel so detached that they couldn't possibly understand?

Loneliness is something that we all feel, but which is almost impossible to admit to. It implies weakness, that we need others, can't look after ourselves. Sometimes, though, that's actually true – we're social animals, called to connect with others at a fundamental level. At other times, we need our space, just to be allowed to be ourselves for a while.

There's no shame in feeling like an outsider. It can be the leg-up that we need to start moving again after a long personal absence. Or it can drag us down further by highlighting how 'outside' of the social world we may feel.

The dark parts of our mind don't allow for rationalisation of such feelings and fears. While we know at some level that our friends wouldn't mind a call to ask for company or even just a chat, we tell ourselves that we're imposing, a nuisance, not good to be around right now. And so we remain alone, lost in our own space.

Plant your feet. Feel the floor. Sit or stand, as you wish. Find a tree if you're outdoors, placing your hand on the trunk, or leaning against it if appropriate. Hold onto a personal object, a pendant or stone.

Feel your body. Feel your connection to the solid things around you. You're still here.

Feel your breath. Is it fast with panic, or caught in gasps as you try to control it? Just visualise your breath, entering and leaving your mouth, like mist on a cold day. It's part of you. You're still breathing.

Feel the loneliness. What is it like? A cold trickle through your veins, a rock in your belly, a skittering panic at the edge of your mind? See it. Name it. Call it out, pull it into view to see where it comes from.

What are you afraid of, when the loneliness bites? Let the words come. No friends, unworthy, useless, unloved ... ?

Hold on to the objects around you – whether the floor under you, tree at your side, or just a chair or table nearby. You are still here.

You know – truly know – that those words are untrue. There are those who love and value you, human and non-human. There are those who understand you, or who appreciate you for your differences. They may not be here right now, but they are there. You can go to them whenever you wish. They may be as glad of a call as you.

But for now, this is your space. Your own, nobody else's. Feel your body. Reach into your own mind to find that part you call 'me' – the uniqueness that is your Self. Nobody else thinks your thoughts, loves what you do, laughs at what you do. Be honest with yourself. No shame or guilt – there's no place for that at this moment.

It doesn't matter if nobody's around right now to see. You're still here.

Now do something. Just for you. Prepare food to nourish yourself, find a book or movie to entertain yourself. Do something that will allow you to move, to focus your thoughts on doing something *for you, now.*

Then take the time to enjoy it. Time for and with yourself.

You may be surprised to find that you can be good company, if you get to know yourself well enough – the good parts and the bad. As any decent friend would.

Allow yourself to be alone. Learn how it feels. Make the space yours, so that it isn't uncontrolled, unknown or fearsome. It's just you.

Then, when you're ready, you can take yourself out into the world, knowing that you're still in there. Challenge yourself – hold on to your own integrity, your strength, while facing that madness of Other People. Allow yourself to smile.

The ground is still beneath you. You're still breathing.

Wasting Time

Clocks slay time ... time is dead as long as it is being clicked off by little wheels; only when the clock stops does time come to life.
– William Faulkner

You know you have to get on with something, to keep busy, to just *be doing* ... but your mind won't let you focus. You can't concentrate for long enough to engage with a task, no matter how simple. Frustration grows, making things worse.

We're always being pushed and pulled, it seems. Constantly busy, with no escape, always jobs to be done, commitments to fulfil, people we're obliged to do things for. It's easy to lose yourself in the hubbub.

Or when you finally do find a spare moment to yourself, you just don't know what to do with it. You've lost yourself. You don't know what *you* want to do. The time flies past and is gone, wasted.

Sometimes it helps to make lists of tasks. Sometimes that makes things worse, as more time is spent organising than actually doing. Lists are guidelines or tools, but they can easily become far more demanding than the tasks they describe.**Allow yourself to know that your life is your own. Your time is your own. *You* decide what to do and when.**

This can be daunting. All of that space in which to move, all of those hours to fill ... remember a time when such a prospect was exciting, to be anticipated. A long vacation, school holidays, simple days off. Try to capture that feeling again.

After all, what is 'wasting' time? What did you do? Some might consider hours spent playing a game (whether computer or sports) to be wasted – but if you enjoyed yourself, were stimulated and amused, that's no different to any other form of entertainment. If pressed, let yourself be inspired by whatever

you did that was 'wasting' – consider it as a story, an adventure that you were part of. If it makes you laugh or smile, it was definitely not lost.

Often, it's your own perception of the value of time that is the difficulty. If you frustrate yourself by sitting about doing nothing, then that's not valuable time spent – you're not relaxing or recharging, you're worrying and making yourself feel worse. If you must do something, even while sitting, consider alternatives that you would enjoy and be glad to look back on at the end of that day. Then do it.

Sometimes it's a matter of finding the energy to go about your tasks. Learn what you're capable of. On one day, you may feel able to push yourself a little more; on another, perhaps less than you would have liked. That's fine. This will balance out.

Yes, you might have obligations, promises made, loved ones to look after. Work with these jobs. Why did you take them on? Are you able to fulfil them? Will the others involved understand if you try to arrange an alternative? Work within that relationship, but remember that you are a part of it as well – equal exchange, not servant and master. If it truly is unbearable, you *are* able to change it. Explore the situation yourself, and be as honest as you can be. No excuses.

The important thing is to ultimately remember that you are alive. Movement is necessary, otherwise you stop or stagnate. Sometimes, you may feel that all you want to do is hide, escape, run away. If this is the case, then heed that warning, pause to rest ... but make the promise to yourself that you will take that time to try and relax, become calm, bring yourself back from the edge. When you're ready, you can resume whatever it was you were doing. At such moments you aren't obliged, you're not being judged – you are taking time for yourself, because you need to. This is important. The challenge here, though, is to not get bogged down in such periods; when rest spills over into laziness, the worries about 'wasting time' will resume.

Honour yourself and your life by 'spending' it as well as you can. We're all human and need to rest and recharge, but we also need to be inspired, stimulated and creative. Find your balance, learn what suits you best.

Keep exploring and challenging – yourself and others along the way.

The Depths

The greatest hazard of all, losing one's self, can occur very quietly in the world, as if it were nothing at all. No other loss can occur so quietly; any other loss – an arm, a leg, five dollars, a wife, etc. – is sure to be noticed. – Søren Kierkegaard

Sometimes there is only despair. Reading about this in self-help books can be unintentionally hilarious, as 'experts' scientifically explore an emotion that is so fundamentally wild, primal, unable to be easily categorised or treated, that it seems almost disappointing that there's no easy cure.

Despair can creep into your soul, insipid, sucking. Or it can bite and hold on. The language of metaphor is the only one that truly approaches this feeling accurately – otherwise it can only be conveyed in screams, yells, groans ... the non-language of soul-deep pain.

And yet, despair is a very human emotion, as we try to understand it. We niggle away, trying to understand our own minds, why we think the way we do. Animals just get on with it. It takes an awful lot to create despair in an animal – they have their own priorities, and self-knowledge doesn't appear to be included.

If one word were to sum up despair, in my experience, it would perhaps be 'why?' *Why* am I feeling this, *why* can't I be happy again? *Why* does nobody understand? *Why* can I only see the world in shades of grey?

Grey is that dullness between dark and light. It has tremendous potential, but it also obscures. Fog, cloud ... something to be penetrated? Or something to be explored?

When you're in the dark pit of darkness that is despair, there is no motivation to *do*. This is where the danger lies. If you stop – that's the end. Despair's most terrible result is suicide. No way out, trapped, no point.

And yet, consider how hard it is to truly *Stop*.

Your body is always moving. Your thoughts are always moving (even if the conscious ones are negative). You don't have total control over this. You are a creature, with instincts and drives. One of these is (believe it or not) to live.

Face your despair. Imagine it however it appears to you – an amorphous grey cloud, a faceless man in black, a huge dog at your side. Face it. And look at it. Why does it look that way? What does it have to say?

If you're able, challenge it. Address it. Scream, cry – it doesn't matter. It may respond, it may not. It's your subconscious.

Consider what your despair is doing to you. How it feels physically and mentally. The heaviness in your stomach, the tears, the unfocused, floating thoughts, the lethargy ... however it feels to you.

If caught in the depths, sometimes it helps to go with it. Lie down somewhere safe (bed is excellent for this, as refuge and healing place).

Move *into* your despair. Don't be afraid – just close your eyes and let it come. Remember, you're in a safe place, protected and held. Swim in it. Let yourself float. Be engulfed. Let the tears come, the sounds of pain.

If you have a loving partner or friend to hold you, and you're comfortable with that, then please do so. A pet at your side may also help. There's no need to be alone in body, but this is something that you have to do yourself.

Yes, it's a battle. But it's not one that you can necessarily overcome with force of arms. Anger just leads to despair. Kicking out just causes more pain.

By learning how your despair feels, as part of you, you can explore it, try to discover what it has to teach you.

Is your despair a defence mechanism? What is it protecting you from? Try to explain to it that it's suffocating you, preventing you from living. Journey with it. Why should spirit/journey companions be animals?

Allow your thoughts to flow. Give the pain a voice – but then do it the honour of listening. This is something so important to you, as it engulfs your life. *Why?*

When you are done, thank your despair. Bid it farewell, as in any other ritual. Then get up, and with as much focus and intention as you can, do something tangible and normal. Making a cup of tea is excellent.

You are still moving.

Human Heroes

No, what he didn't like about heroes was that they were usually suicidally gloomy when sober and homicidally insane when drunk.
– Terry Pratchett

Who inspires you? Who do you look at and admire, smile at their words and deeds, or seek help from?

Are they real or fictional? Friend or relative? Known to you personally? A celebrity or a regular, everyday person?

Now consider why this is. What has that person got, what are they doing, that you haven't got, or don't do? They're a person, just like you.

Imagine them when times get tough. What do they do? We don't often see others when they're in times of crisis. Folk tend to become secluded, retreat inside, remove themselves from the gaze of the wider world. Or alternatively, battle on, pasting a smile to their face so that others never know.

Sound familiar?

We're all human. Living our lives as best we can. Imagine that you are admired in the same way – reverse your role with this inspiring individual. Does it help?

What are they doing that you wish you could do? How can you do that? How would you do that differently, adding your own personality, your own skills and perspective? How would you inspire others?

Do you already? Are you aware of it? Do your children admire their Mum/Dad, or your friends wish for your coping skills?

Everyone has value. Everyone, without exception. The challenge is to express it, live it, be honourable and true to yourself.

Times can be difficult. Acknowledge this. Know that you can ride the waves – you've done so before. Take that inspiration from others and make it your own. Do Your Thing, your way.

We all have that same Spirit, that inspiration, the flame

inside us that keeps us going. It's just a matter of finding it and nurturing it. Especially when the dark times try to smother it.

Sometimes it's impossible to see your own value, your spark that you bring to the world. But others can. Know when to listen, truly listen – and honour them enough to believe what they say.

I've found that there are some people that you just have an affinity towards, and are naturally comfortable with. These are the people who guide us, or even need our guidance.

I have a lovely son who has a problem with IV drug use. His problem has turned my life upside down, with the lying, cheating prison visits and gut-wrenching worry and wretchedness. Yet we have a very close bond.

*A shaman once told me that when it is our time to come back onto this world, we can make a choice about who we want to be influential in our lives and to help us with our journey. I jokingly said that I would not have chosen my son; she told me that **he** may have chosen **me** to deal with and support him. That thought was quite awe-inspiring, and completely changed my attitude.*

Beverley

Moving with the Tides

The next time you walk outside on a clear night and see the moon smiling down at you, think of Neil Armstrong and give him a wink.
– The family of Neil Armstrong, first man to walk on the Moon

We are all creatures of the Earth, this blue-green planet that we call home. Yet we are subject to the push and pull of our nearest satellite, with every culture holding awareness of the Moon, with many interlinking mythologies surrounding its effect on our lives. Our relationship with the Moon continues today, as we explore and discover new and awesome aspects of this small sphere that inspire and encourage us to step further out into the wider Universe – both of science and story.

Categorised by scientific exploration, tacitly understood in our blood, these tides affect us deeply. Any Emergency Service data demonstrates the fluctuations of our lives as the planet moves and we lose control – the word 'lunacy' speaks volumes. The tale of the werewolf runs through many societies, howling the hidden wildness beneath our skin.

As Pagans, we hold the Moon sacred, recognising the ties between it – so many miles away – and us. Simply standing, watching. Whether the Man in the Moon, or the Lady, so we realise there is more to be known, within and without.

From New Moon, to Full Moon, to New Moon again, so the cycle turns – and we turn with it.

For a full lunar cycle, take time each night to step outside and look up. See the progression of the Moon, from the first crescent through to the last. How does it feel to witness each phase? How is the Dark Moon different to the Full?

Observe your moods from day to night through a complete lunar cycle – and then another. Are you affected by the dark, the light, or the transitional times in-between? Do you have

more energy at a particular time, or feel lethargic at another?
Mark moods and phases on a chart or calendar, if it helps to
remind you. See your connection to the wider world as it turns.

In the shadows where I walk
No one has the time to talk
No one stops to pass the day
They just glance at your eyes and turn right away.

In the shadows where I exist
You're just a body on somebody's list
Nobody bothers to know your name
Just a bit player in another's game.

In the shadows where I hide
I can bury the loneliness deep inside
I can look at the sun and maybe pretend
That someone somewhere will one day call me friend.

In the shadows where I stand
The world passes me by in a blur and
I'm alone again in a crowded place
I have no voice, I have no face.

In the shadows where the world is grey
I stand alone whilst others play
I know somehow I am to blame
For why they won't let me join their game.

In the shadows I make a choice
I decide I'm gonna find myself a voice
I'll stand at the crossroads and scream my name loud
No longer in shadows but strong now and proud.
Tony

Spirit

The Circle

You're alive. Do something. – Barbara Hall

Earth, air, fire and water. 'Tangible' elements, everyday essentials to life. As Pagans, these are central to the structure of our practice, the four corners of our whole.

Spirit is both the central point and the circle itself, all-encompassing, crucial. The thing inside you that keeps you going; the things outside of you that you connect with, but which are themselves living parts of the world that you walk on, are part of.

Many Pagans remember when they first started to really understand and conceptualise the idea of 'spirit in everything'. This can cause a huge change in perspective. How do you cut down a branch from a living tree? How do you eat the meat of a cow, or use cosmetics which contain animal matter?

How do you differentiate yourself, the importance of your own Spirit, from these others? Why is one more – or less – important?

Consider your Self. Your body, yes, but also what's inside. Who are YOU? Try to view yourself as an outsider would, without judgement, just interest. Be curious. Explore yourself. There's good and bad, of course. But what's really YOU? What's been implanted onto you, that you can actually identify as 'other' ... and perhaps get rid of?

Magic

Magic is believing in yourself, if you can do that, you can make anything happen. – Johann Wolfgang von Goethe

Modern Paganism can be synonymous with magic. Witchcraft and wizardry, cauldrons and moonlight – the line between popular culture and actual practice blurs very easily.

But magic is not simply forcing things to happen. It's not making the Universe conform to your demands. It's not escaping into fantasy.

One of the most famous definitions of magic is Dion Fortune's: 'the art of changing consciousness at will.'

Changing consciousness. Not performing supernatural acts, or going outside Nature. Changing the consciousness of yourself (and potentially others) in order to accomplish your intention.

Sometimes it seems a lovely idea, to be able to snap your fingers and alter your mood on demand. That's Hollywood magic – illusory, superficial. We need to look deeper.

The 'art' itself is key. Finding the magic within you in order to create change.

Let's formulate a spell.

What do you want to happen? What is your goal, right now? Keep it simple and personal. Do you want to heal yourself? To simply feel better for now?

How are you able to accomplish this? It's just you. If you have the simplest of tools to hand, you can use them – lighting a candle can inspire – but again, keep it simple.

You already have the elements to hand to centre yourself. Flex your muscles, your body, physical form standing on earth. Breathe the air through your lungs. Lick your lips to feel the moisture in your mouth, preparing you to speak. Feel the fire of your blood, your life, your inspiration held inside, ready.

State your intention. "I want ... " "I promise ... " "I resolve to try ... " Be honest, use words that you truly mean. You don't need flowery, formal language – be simple. Know what you are saying is true.

Helpful spirits or deities may be listening. It might just be you. Make your resolution to yourself. Feel the words, the energy of your determination, become reality as you speak the words. You are making magic.

Psychologically-speaking, you may simply be informing your subconscious what you want to happen. You are making a statement. Now you must follow it through – your effort is required.

How do you feel for formulating this intention, for speaking it aloud? Has your consciousness changed, your mood? Do you feel hopeful, excited, a bit silly?

Now move forward and make your words – your spell – come true.

Love

Have you ever been in love? Horrible isn't it? It makes you so vulnerable. It opens your chest and it opens up your heart and it means that someone can get inside you and mess you up. – Neil Gaiman

Love is a tricky one. Please don't turn away now – this isn't going to be fluffy, New-Age endearments or social-media style platitudes. This is simple, basic.

Love is wonderful, certainly – when it's on the upswing. But love can hurt, more deeply than anything.

Love can be the catalyst for breakdown, mental collapse, and the ensuing physical debasement. Simply lack of caring for yourself, the loss of self-love (and esteem, and confidence).

If we can't love ourselves, it's so hard to love others, even in a friendly or familial way.

So, you feel an affinity for the Pagan path? Perhaps openly call yourself Pagan? Consider the non-human life-forms around you. The flora and fauna in your garden or local neighbourhood. Your pets.

Life seems to be simpler for them, doesn't it? But non-animals certainly get depressed – when they're abandoned, lose their reason for living, and other such entirely understandable circumstances.

When we're lost, we're back in our basic animal states. We have no connection, no focus or goal. We've lost ourselves.

Even connecting with one other person at this time can help.

Reach out. Make yourself do so. A friend is good, but also there are those who won't judge in any way – a favourite tree, your dog or cat (or other animal companion).

Verbalise if you can. Let your story pour out, in gushes or short spurts. Or just let the tears come. Connect with a touch.

They may not understand quite what you're going through (which may be why you've pushed other human people away), but they will see that you're trying to connect to another living being.

Let yourself be open to that. Let another spirit be there with you, support you for a little while in simple companionship.

You are not alone.

Being deeply loved by someone gives you strength, while loving someone deeply gives you courage. – Lao Tzu

Oh, Gods ...

I know God won't give me anything I can't handle. I just wish he didn't trust me so much. – Mother Theresa

As Pagan folk, we often look to the deities of our ancestors, our tribes, to guide us on our own contemporary paths. We've seen some in these pages already, but let us look more deeply now.

Who do you consider your 'personal' deity, God and/or Goddess? Why is this? What drew you to them originally?

How do you connect with them, honour them, work with them? It doesn't matter if you consider yourself 'lapsed' or 'it's been too long' – remember a rite that you undertook, just you and your Gods, together. The flicker of candles, scents in the air, charged atmosphere ... remember.

Or just think back to a time when you felt close to Deity. At a sacred place, perhaps. Or did you call on them in the street, and they were there? A simple walk through the woods ...

Your Gods know you. You have that connection, that relationship. You can call on them. Rock bottom is a time of need, and sometimes all you need is to be held.

Your Gods are not a Pagan 'tick-box'. They are with you, part of your life, as much as you let them. Mother and Father, Lord and Lady ... or just another person, who might understand if you honoured them by asking.

When the black dog follows me around, I find that getting away from the pressures of modern life really helps. Times around the full moon are usually the best for me.

I like to hide perfectly still in the woods, listening to the sound of the waterfall nearby, feeling my heart pumping the blood around my body and bathing in the monochromic light of the moon, my Lady, shining through the trees.

Occasionally I'll hear the rustle of a small creature in the under-growth, the bark of a dog fox or the cry of an owl hunting in the dark. This is truly getting 'back to basics' and reminds me where I came from – that I am part of nature, not above it. I like to think of it as a cleansing shower for my soul.

Tony

Others

This guy's walking down the street when he falls in a hole. The walls are so steep he can't get out. A doctor passes by and the guy shouts up, 'Hey you. Can you help me out?' The doctor writes a prescription, throws it down in the hole and moves on. Then a priest comes along and the guy shouts up, 'Father, I'm down in this hole can you help me out?' The priest writes out a prayer, throws it down in the hole and moves on. Then a friend walks by. 'Hey, Joe, it's me can you help me out?' And the friend jumps in the hole. Our guy says, 'Are you stupid? Now we're both down here.' The friend says, 'Yeah, but I've been down here before and I know the way out.' – Leo McGarry, 'The West Wing'.

Sometimes, the hardest thing to face is those close to you. Family, friends – those who love you.

When you're in the dark places, you may not be able to understand why those others choose to stay so close to you, with your multitude of faults and problems.

You may feel obliged to be cheerful, to present the mask of 'I'm fine'. This doesn't fool those who know you well.

The urge to hide grows, as you're unable to bear the thought that others may break through to see your pain. Shame and guilt add to the burden – but this is unnecessary. These aspects of the darkness can be recognised as false, and fought through.

It's true that personal darkness isn't something that everyone can understand or accept. You may well find out who your true friends are, as those who are themselves frightened by your experiences gradually fade away, no longer staying in touch. This doesn't prove that you're the cause of their pain – just that they have their own darkness to face in due course. We all do.

Those who choose to remain through it all may not be able to understand exactly what you're going through – but they do know that you're worth the time and effort. That is their decision.

Honour your friends and loved ones for remaining, for being there with you. Sometimes this can be in the form of simply being yourself. You don't have to put up a false front – let them help you through, just by their presence.

While it can be easy for your internal monologue to constantly tell you how bad things are, a friend is less easily to trick. They can expose those ideas to the light of reason, showing you truths that you may have been unable to see through the gloom. They bring fresh insights, energy and support. Is this what you were truly hiding from?

Yes, it's sometimes necessary to be alone. But you know that at others times, all you truly need is someone with you. Find those friends, and let them in.

When you can, ask them if they'd like to know how it feels to be in the dark – not to share the pain, but to help them under-stand. It can also help to put things into words. If they are able, you can tell your story as they hold on.

You might even strike a chord that you never realised was there. Others hide their pain just as well, if not better. Join together in shared experiences – as you have before.

You may wish to specifically ask them not to judge. These are confusing times, troubling experiences. They may be confused as to why you feel these things, not knowing what to do to help. Tell them. A cup of tea, a hug, just company that listens, so that you're not alone. Sometimes you may need a distraction; at other times, a companion as you face things head-on. Be honest.

And when you've had enough, when you are working hard, determined to come out the other side, know that these partners, companions and loved ones will be there for you.

You are valued.

Ever felt alone in the dark
Even though there is light?
Ever heard the black dog bark
Even though you smile in delight?

That brave face you're putting on
The automatic reply – 'I'm fine'
I'm still here when the facade's gone
I see passed the simple line.

Join with me as we welcome the Goddess
Join with me in Her loving embrace
I may not make your problems less
I may not know the troubles you face

But together we'll see it through
The Goddess' support all the way
That beautiful smile will finally come true
The black dog held far at bay

Remember you are never on your own
If you ever want to talk, scream or shout
I vow on Maiden, Mother, Crone
We're always here to help you out.

Vix

Hiding

All is part of nature, but much of the realm of nature is 'occult,' that is, hidden. – Doreen Valiente

Intellectually, we all know that life is about balance, about the black and white, give and take, good times and bad.

Subconsciously, we know it's not as simple as that.

We can't just 'get over it'. I've never quite learned how to 'just cheer up'. And what exactly does a 'stiff upper lip' achieve?

We're all hiding in some form. The world is fearsome, daunting, challenging. But we are in it, part of it. As Pagans, consciously connecting to it, working to explore our relationship with it. We are 'it'.

This is not a matter of waving a magic wand to make things better. 'Better' may not actually be an improvement for you. Change is the central constant to life, and once we realise that at a deep, fundamental level, we can begin to consciously change too.

We face the darkness as much as the light. Both hide and expose, both are unavoidable, inexorable. We are a mixture of both, in body, mind and spirit, made up of many subtle shades.

So ask yourself:

What are you hiding from? What do you hide?

What would happen if you were to step into the light?

What if people were willing to step into the darkness to truly see you?

How do you want to live? How can you begin to achieve this, what steps can you take?

Now start to move.

Balance

The word 'happiness' would lose its meaning if it were not balanced by sadness. – C.G. Jung

Life can seem like a balancing act, walking a knife-edge between sanity and madness, dark and light, normal and ... what?

When we've been to extremes, it can be hard to gain perspective on what's 'normal', in terms of society's expectations. 'Normal' can seem pretty insane at times, after all. Wouldn't we rather be individuals, with our own personal, learned experiences? After all, how can anyone understand *me*?

We each walk our own path, true – but as an inevitable, indivisible part of a larger whole. As Pagans, we see ourselves not just as part of the human species, but as a part of the life on this planet in its entirety – if not of the greater Universe.

We balance our own lives with those of our ancestors, our fellow humans, our fellow living creatures, our environment. That's a formidable juggling act – but as we are part of each and all of these, so they are part of us.

We make change, for ourselves and for the wider world. Our experiences are part of this, no matter if they are perceived as good or bad. The 'wounded healer' learns from his or her challenges. We cannot always be in the darkness – or the light – but walk between the two consciously, as best we can with awareness and intention.

A small act of ritual, of magic, can speak to our subconscious and create, change, help.

Find a torque – one of the Celtic-style bangles that is an open ring to be worn on the wrist. This can be as ornate or simple as you wish: from a copper magnetic bracelet that aids medical conditions, to a beautiful tooled piece of jewellery.

On the evening of the New Moon, sit in a place that is sacred

to you. A personal altar space, a garden, wild wood or seashore – somewhere you won't be disturbed. Lay out formal ritual space if you wish and are able, but ultimately all this small rite needs is you and the torque, as an object of focus.

Consciously welcome the elements to the space, to be present and bear witness to your act. The earth beneath you and in your body; the air around and in your breath; the fire of the setting sun and in your life; and the water of the seas that surround you and in your blood.

Be aware of the tides of the moon. You are there at the dark time, of beginnings and endings, a liminal space where magic can be worked and change can be set in motion.

Feel the darkness within you, lapping at your own internal shores. Let tears flow, if you need to. Breathe deeply, holding the strength of what you are doing.

Consider the torque. Really focus on it, examine it, turn it in your hands to view it with every one of your senses. A simple piece of metal, touched by many before you. It is a ring, but not joined – the connection is broken, with two ends facing each other. Our ancestors wore these as symbols of power and strength.

See the balance in the two ends of the torque. They may be adorned with figures facing each other, as was traditional in artefacts that we have found buried. They may be simple and plain.

Recognise and honour the power of the elements within this bracelet – the earth from which it was taken, the fire that forged it, the water that quenched it, air that cooled it. The inspiration that went into it. Now it is here to help and inspire you.

Set your intention. As you wear this torque for the duration of the next moon-cycle, you will feel its balance – in the elements within it and within you. The two ends face each other, unjoined but united, balancing as they face each other.

The ring is created by including that unknown space within, that mystery that is held in the place where dark and light meet. Not everything is visible or tangible, but it is *there*.

You stand in that liminal space, that place between. You hold the balance of dark and light, the earth and air, the fire and water. Each complements and opposes each other, in a constant dance. So your darkness reflects your light, allowing you to live apparently broken, but actually whole – and with purpose.

Thank those who came to bear witness to your actions. Take the time to sit and reflect, to ground yourself again before heading home.

When you need to over the next month, feel the metal at your wrist and remember the energy of this evening, the focus of your own will, your determination and energy. Take strength from it as you need to.

This rite can be performed as often as you wish, reaffirming your intention, with the solidity of the torque acting as a simple reminder and inspiration.

The grey days are the worst. Everything is still going on in the world, but seen through a filter, a semi-sepia toned fog of dull, brooding clouds. Nothing can be done, because nothing is worth doing. Part of me wants to just sit, or lie under the thickest duvet I can find. Protected from the outside, but also stuck there with what's inside – the voices in my mind, telling me how worthless I am, useless, hated, despised, unwanted ... a constant tirade of loathing, that seems designed to stop me from ever functioning again.

I've never really been able to understand where this comes from, nor what purpose it serves. Medical professionals and helpful books suggest that it's a protective mechanism, an animal instinct left over from our genetic heritage, something to do with the 'fight or flight' response. I don't entirely understand that (especially in those moments of self-hate). I suspect that it's another aspect of so-called 'mental illness' that the scientific professionals are still exploring. They have a long way to go – the target is tricky to pin down. Subduing it with tranquillisers doesn't really solve anything; existing day-to-day at a basic level of functional catatonia can't really be called 'living'.

"So why are you putting yourself through this?" my brain asked conversationally one day.

I was surprised. My subconscious isn't normally so chatty – or so coherent.

"I don't know, I can't seem to pull myself out of it."

"But you know who you are, how you feel when you're properly yourself. Can't you aim for that?"

"I do, but it's like battling through thick snow or fog. Or beating my fists against a glass wall, impenetrable – I can see the world going on, and people can see me, but I can't make myself heard. Not my real self, anyway. I feel like I'm screaming inside my mind, but nobody can see to come and help."

"You have days to yourself, yes? With good company, safe at home?"

" ... Yes. But I find it so hard to enjoy them. I'm always worrying about something – money, work. My brain is always telling me that there's something I **should** be doing, which I'm not, so I'm bad. And there's the circle, of can't do because I'm so busy telling myself that I **can't** do what I **should**. Argh.""So stop it. Break the circle."

"What?"

"You're always doing something. Do that. Don't worry about the deadlines – you're aware of them, they'll get sorted. Or you'll have to explain that you're not well and have to ask for a few more days, then focus and get on with the job. But you're still in control."

"Am I?"

"Do your thing. Do what you want to be doing for a while. Enjoy it. Be frivolous. Write a silly story. Draw a bad picture. Go walking, anywhere. It doesn't matter. Not everything is life or *death. Take some time just for **you**, and tell the worries to go hang. They're stopping you enjoying your life, and you know that you have to take a stand against that. Take yourself back."*

"But ... "

"No. Try it. Stop letting yourself be told. You know yourself. Hold on to that. Be you."

I was flabbergasted. So simple ... could I really do this? I remembered living without the worry, just enjoying life. Could I do it again?

I wandered into the bathroom, to clean up in readiness for dressing (in something that I liked) and seeing what I felt like doing next. That thought in itself seemed unbelievably freeing. Could I do this? Really?

Looking into the mirror. Seeing, truly seeing, my own face, my eyes. My smile, at last.

The black dog has fled. In its place is a cat with red fur, ready to walk forward.

Cat

(February 2013)

Moon Books invites you to begin or deepen your encounter with Paganism, in all its rich, creative, flourishing forms.